THE SEVEN ETERNAL LAWS OF SUCCESS

THE SEVEN ETERNAL LAWS OF SUCCESS

PERSONAL AND PROFESSIONAL DEVELOPMENT GUIDE

BLAISE NZETCHOANG N.

Rev. date: 07/07/2020

To order additional copies of this book, contact:
Xlibris
1-888-795-4274
www.Xlibris.com
Orders@Xlibris.com
814441

CONTENTS

ABOUT THE AUTHOR

Who Is Blaise Nzetchoang N.?

BLAISE POSSESSES A certain charisma, undoubtedly because he exudes a deeply reassuring quiet strength. He is a sociable, loving, communicative, extroverted person. Greatly appreciative of harmony and justice-loving, he is willing to make great efforts to keep the peace. He is a creative aesthete who is good with his hands and often pursues artistic pastimes. As a child, he was deeply influenced by his family and distressed by any parental discord. He was a tender, affectionate, helpful boy and quickly became independent and responsible. With his paternal spirit, he is a dream elder brother who diligently cared for his little brothers and sisters. His adoptive parents saw this very quickly, and his sense of responsibility made him trustworthy. Last, he is a gifted communicator. He is eloquent, persuasive, curious, adaptable, and lively.

What Does He Like to Do?

Blaise likes to talk, communicate, and discuss. He displays a real penchant for argumentation and brainteasers. He excels in business and economics and is interested in discussions, where he displays outstanding language skills. Like a chameleon, he enjoys blending in with his surroundings and speaking with the accent of wherever he is. A good ear and a knack for learning foreign languages help him achieve this. Perhaps the other side of the coin is a taste for idle chatter and a tendency to exaggerate or embellish the truth: the main thing for him is to be admired, entertain, and, in a word, be the center of attention.

A man with refined senses, he is a true epicurean in his appreciation of worldly pleasures. A fine dinner with friends or family—where he participates as a true gourmet by rolling up his sleeves and getting involved, especially in selecting the best wines—is a treasured moment for him. But he must be careful not to become a prisoner of his senses.

What Does He Do?

He can be found in university classrooms engaged in long courses of study because he strives for intellectual enrichment. His sense of responsibility has led him down the path of politics (from association head to the highest positions depending on the scope of his ambitions). Languages, writing, and oral expression, which are sources of satisfaction for him, have naturally led him to professions that require these talents, such as translator, interpreter, representative, guide, lawyer, and public speaker. Nevertheless, business is his field of choice, and regardless of the professional sector, he seeks out responsibility.

Monique Tatiana Koko E.
August 27, 2011

PREFACE

YOUR PAST CIRCUMSTANCES may determine who you are, so your future depends on the decisions you make today. No matter what the circumstances of life want to make of you, stand tall and stand your ground until you are living your dream life.

I know a man from a poor family born in 1986 in Western Cameroon in Central Africa. His father was married to several women. His mother was the last one. He was his mother's fourth child, an unfavorable position. His father died young, and his memories of him were unclear, almost insignificant. He died in a car accident when the boy was about two years old. His mother used to put him on her back in his early years when she plied her trade as a peddler, knocking on many doors of downtown administrative offices, selling a little bit of everything. She was strong and persistent, always putting together a series of exceptional pitches to describe the quality of her goods. She did not take no for an answer; through her powers of persuasion, she never returned with the same number of items that she had left home with. She went out into the unknown every morning without an attack strategy or a map when she went to the offices, and she always managed to sell something to support her four children. Sun, rain, cold weather, and fatigue never stopped her. She went out every morning, hoping to make some money.

At the crack of dawn, she went out to her tent outside the house to fry fritters and prepare beans and corn porridge that she sold until about 9:00 a.m., when all the local students who ate breakfast at her house had to be in class from Monday to Friday.

At about 10:00 a.m., she was on her way to her other business in the downtown area until administrative offices closed. She could travel more than ten kilometers going from office to office.

In the afternoon, when her chances of making sales had been exhausted, it was time to go home. Before returning, she made sure to shop for the needs of the evening and sometimes for the next day's business because she did not have a refrigerator or freezer to store products for several days. Once she had purchased her groceries and supplies, she went home. Upon arrival, she needed to take care of the family and prepare food for her children—if she had the chance to see all of them come home that day.

One of the brothers of the young man, whose first name was Merlin, caused his mother great distress by his constantly delinquent habits. He will end up having lived more of his life in prisons than the family home. Merlin ruined the old woman's efforts by causing her tremendous pain. She tried to help in every way she could, but his addiction to theft was so deeply ingrained that he paid for it with his life after several instances of vigilante justice left him with injuries, infections, broken bones, and concussions.

The young boy's other brother Pergolès tried his luck in West Africa. He ended up in jail. While in a prison far from the whole family, the mother managed to send him money without any guarantee that he would receive it. He was released from prison four years later and was returned home. To everyone's surprise, he was no longer the same. He showed signs of mental illness. He had become a frightening, disoriented shadow of himself. He no longer wanted to do anything with his life. He seemed as if he had come face-to-face with Lucifer himself. He wandered the streets from morning to night and sometimes left the family home. He would end up in another city without having told anyone, causing a panic and anxiety most heavily borne by his mother. Four years later, he decided to kill himself. He deprived himself of food, water, and other nourishment until he died. His mother felt tremendous grief. She did not understand the ordeal she was going through with her children. Only two remained—my sister and I, her young boy.

The boy's mother lived through every day with the sweat, fear, and anxiety caused by the uncertainty of what the next day would bring. The future looked bleak because the present was a painful march through poverty, loneliness, fear, and insecurity. Although everyday life weighed on her shoulders, something, nevertheless, gave her hope for the future.

She was already facing even more severe financial difficulties when her husband died; she felt that the environment was not conducive to the young boy's upbringing. The eponymous nephew of the boy's mother suggested giving him an opportunity. He took the boy to live with him in a province of the country far away from his family and hometown. The boy's cousin had just been recruited into a tobacco company as an agronomist. The young husband decided to give the boy a family environment suitable for his upbringing. The boy was so young and looking for a father; all his life, he called him "Dad." He left his family for a fresh start. It was the beginning of a new story that would make a man of him. The young man, although not highly intelligent, was studious, hardworking, and helpful. He remembered where he came from and knew that this opportunity had to be taken very seriously. He dreamed of becoming an important member of society. He was full of ambition and always sought out opportunities at his schools to display and develop his charisma and leadership ability. He knew that, to succeed, he had to fight much harder than everyone else because he had no margin for error—his adoptive parents had made that clear to him whenever the opportunity arose. Aware of the burden on his shoulders at such a young age, he swore to himself that his children would not experience the same fate because few can emerge from such a difficult childhood unscathed. He dreamed of building a financial empire, but he had to start from scratch and achieve his goals despite very unfavorable socioeconomic circumstances.

A situation disrupted his life but, this time, in a good way: He met his classmate Tatiana. She came to fill the void in the life of a boy who had become a young man. She was a brilliant young woman with a strong personality. She radiated the light that he needed.

They were young, innocent, and very much in love. They understood each other and decided to spend their life together, sharing the dream of making the world a better place with their companies.

This story has left its mark on me and raised many questions about the human condition and the role we must play in this world. You must refuse to be a prisoner of your current circumstances and take steps to make changes.

In fact, the story of the boy is the story of my life, and I am happy to share it with you so that anyone reading understands that luck does not exist: It simply occurs when preparation meets opportunity.

ACKNOWLEDGMENTS

I DEDICATE THIS BOOK to my mother, Jeanne, and sister, Sylviane; to my adoptive parents, Clémentine and Flobert Nzetchoang; to my mother-in-law, Olive, for her prayers and her love; and to my three boys, Ivan Blessing, Emmanuel Dawson, and Marc-Olivier. Many thanks to Minister Stéphane Gagné of the Église Baptiste Évangélique Vie nouvelle and Annie Bruneau of Carrefour Santé Nutrition, both in Joliette, for collaborating in the release of this book. From the bottom of my heart, I thank the queen of my heart, Tatiana, for her unconditional love and being in my life. I thank God for His infinite grace and love. I am in His service. May His blessings bring success to all who read this book.

Blaise Nzetchoang N.

INTRODUCTION

I HAVE DEVELOPED MY entrepreneurial skills for more than a decade. One thing I learned from this long ceaseless learning is that entrepreneurship is 10 percent inspiration and 90 percent perspiration. You can, therefore, see why more than 90 percent of the population work for the 10 percent. This may sound unfair, but the sad reality is that the 90 percent are *incapable* of doing what others do to earn the privileges of a dream life. You need to be *capable* to bring together more than one asset if you want to attain your dreams and goals on this earth. For the most part, creators and inventors, great business leaders, heads of state, and the big names in music have taken this path.

One day, when I was twenty-two years old, I was traveling by bus to meet a potential business partner to consider commercial intermediation projects for cocoa and coffee. During the trip, a man boarded the bus promoting audio CDs about motivation and entrepreneurship. He was selling bus passengers a CD about what it means to be *capable*. I was captivated by the title of the audio CD and the concepts covered in it. For many years, I listened and relistened to the same CD to burn these concepts into my brain. For more than a decade, I worked on being *capable* based on the terms of the CD I had purchased from this traveling peddler at a meager price (which was rather high for me during a period of hardship). I have come a long way and tried to apply these laws of success. I want to share my business process and experience with anyone starting from the bottom but yearning to make their dreams a reality, anyone who is eager to achieve success and become wealthy.

The word *capable* is a set of letters that, interpreted differently, are full of crucial concepts for success. Have you ever heard anyone tell you that he or she is *capable* of this or that? After such an assertion, you should conclude that the person has a mastery of the subject and the means to achieve his or her ends. This book will help you do more than merely pursue projects—it will help you achieve *success* by pursuing them differently from everyone else.

We will focus on the basics of business success because such an undertaking requires a mastery of skills that we will study in the next chapters. You will learn many concepts and recipes in books written by businesspeople. But this book is different; it is the result of an ingenuous business initiative that could have cost me my *freedom* and family. I saw no sign of success, but today, although my bank accounts and material assets are not what I had anticipated, I am even richer than I would ever have imagined. The wealth I am talking about is the experience of my many failures and countless disappointments, from which I have always risen and from which I will continue to rise. I always come back stronger because of my unshakeable faith and resilience. I could have earned millions in business in the past, but I might have lost my soul and not have become who I am.

The *goal* of this book is to equip project leaders, entrepreneurs, professionals, and students to be *capable* of doing more than just pursue projects—they will be able to change the world.

You will no longer be the same person by the end of this book, and it will have nothing to do with your education, annual income, or the size of your businesses.

TO REMEMBER

INTRODUCTION

*T*HE SEVEN ETERNAL *Laws of Success* is a book for anyone who yearns to achieve success, reach the top, and achieve what is impossible in the eyes of men and women of little faith. It will help you acquire knowledge, develop a positive mental attitude, love, cultivate patience and perseverance, define a clear and precise *purpose* and goals, live freely according to your instincts, and increase your daily energy. It will make you a *capable* entrepreneur—a different kind of person who inspires trust.

THE LAW OF KNOWLEDGE

Knowledge comes with training,
but expertise comes with practice.

OVER THE COURSE of my studies, I acquired general knowledge in many subjects, such as French, English, the humanities, mathematics, the physical sciences, history, and geography. I was more interested in mathematics and the physical sciences. I liked the constant search for concrete solutions and the thought exercises that equations involved.

Theoretical and Practical Knowledge

Learning the concepts of a discipline is essential for mastering it. It takes many hours, weeks, and even years of devotion and learning. Yes, it is important to learn the theories related to a discipline or profession in books or through academic teachings. Many people want to succeed in fields where they do not know the ingredients; understanding a discipline and acquiring enough knowledge requires patience, time, and effort. Courage is a factor that will greatly help you achieve this despite the obstacles because, believe me, they will come at you from a variety of angles, even from where you do not expect them. Keep in mind that acquiring knowledge through learning is the beginning of success, but theoretical learning alone is not enough; otherwise, your financial markets teacher would possess one of the world's great fortunes.

Later at university, I selected economics and applied business management. For a few years, I sought the secrets of entrepreneurship in books and during my education, especially with the theorists who were my teachers. I learned many things but not enough to have the courage to go into business. I began a self-directed learning process that developed my resourcefulness and flair for research. I read all the books about business start-ups and successful people and autobiographies that I could get my hands on. I surrounded myself with people who develop businesses on a daily basis and came to the following conclusion: Entrepreneurship is 10 percent inspiration and 90 percent perspiration. You can have all the theoretical knowledge and ideas necessary to create and develop the best business, product, and service, but it all becomes a reality through the work of continuous daily practices. The best always learn from the best through observation, analysis, and above all, action.

What if you could not only work on learning theoretical knowledge but also practice what you learn every day—not for money, but to be the best, be immersed in the dynamics of the process? Knowledge comes with training, but expertise comes with practice.

I am an expert in *leadership*. This assertion makes sense if you have acquired theoretical knowledge but especially tried-and-true practical know-how that attests to your expertise. Take a look around: You will surely see people with international success in many fields. But if you listen carefully to them, you notice that their stories do not come down to the accumulation of multiple degrees in one or more fields but rather to the practice of knowledge acquired either through observation or trial and error. Nothing can defeat a mind that is determined—I would even say obsessed—with such a process. In this first chapter on *knowledge*, I would obviously like to emphasize the importance of *observing*, *analyzing*, and *practicing* until you have mastered your subject and field. You may not know how to explain it in the right words, but you will, nevertheless, know how to convey it in practice and by example.

Many people wait for the end of their studies in a discipline before they get started. I am not against a formal education, but I think differently. If you want to be a dentist, here's my recommendation: Pay a few hundred dollars to a dentist and observe him for a few days or weeks to watch him do his job and manage the tiniest details of the profession, such as stress management, clients, and so on. Observe and listen to the emotions expressed and the reactions of the dentist and those who assist him. Jot down your findings and come back to them several times to think it over. Come back to it some time later and really ask yourself whether that's what you want to do for the rest of your life. Are you ready to go through that every day? This exercise could be done with many professions. You should only decide to enroll in a school or project and embrace a field after going through this process.

I began my career as an entrepreneur in several fields. One of the most memorable was selling telecommunications products. I spent my first day in the field observing my *leader* for the day working. After a few days, I quickly realized that this was not what I wanted to do over the next few years, not even to pay the bills. Another area I tried out was financial advising. I loved the practical on-the-job training with someone who was quite experienced in the field. The training consisted of observing and learning various approaches. The advisor talked about personal finances and possible solutions he and the company could provide customers to improve their financial situations. I asked him if that's what I would do all the time with clients, and he said yes. He provided clients with a financial education related to their various situations. It was both exciting and informative for someone who was eager to understand a world rich in possibilities but who had poor access to accurate, simplified, and immediately actionable information. The further along I was in the process, the clearer my decision became.

Here are some of the thought-provoking questions in this chapter:

1. What do you want to do as a career for the rest of your life?
2. Do you have the minimum knowledge to get going? If so, *get started*. If not, do you know how and where to acquire it?
3. Do you have contacts whom you can observe engaging in different aspects of the profession?
4. Does it involve a long expensive process? If so, keep thinking it over. If not, *get started*.

5. Will I be independent or dependent when I complete the process?
6. Can I give it a try without necessarily committing in the long term or losing large sums of money?
7. Am I limited in the short, medium, or long term by my level of education, origins, or culture? If so, keep thinking it over. If not, *get started*.
8. Am I in a continuous learning process that improves my knowledge and fosters my creativity? If not, is that what I'm looking for? If so, *get started*.
9. Am I limited in space and time? Am I limited in my income?
10. Can I decide which people I want to partner with? If so, *get started*. If not, who am I looking for? Should I compromise my values?

As you will see, reflecting on these issues is beneficial to you, regardless of whether you are an employee or entrepreneur. But this book is more designed to help project developers and entrepreneurs take a *step* toward their destiny. Here is a word of encouragement for entrepreneurs and project developers: There is no small opportunity because it all depends on your ability to imbue it with a value commensurate with your ambitions. Are you *capable* of that? If so, what follows can make you the best version of yourself. If not, the next chapters will make you into someone who is an eternally *capable* person who breaks norms and has a story that is an inspiration for future generations.

Self-Knowledge

I cannot broach the acquisition and mastery of knowledge without underscoring the importance of self-knowledge. Knowing yourself is a major asset that propels you to the height of your ambitions. If you knew yourself as well as you claim to know others, you would feel that their most reprehensible acts deserve a little indulgence. Do you know yourself well enough as a person? If, in addition to knowing what you want to do, how to do it, and even whom to do it with, you had a real knowledge of yourself, wouldn't you avoid tremendous frustration and much wasted time? It is a major asset to know your strengths and weaknesses, understand them, accept them, and work with them without being frustrated about the smallest trifling details that hinder your creative spirit. Moreover, knowing the strengths and weaknesses of your work team is also crucial if your goal is to make it a *winning* team. You can know what to demand from whom and when and how to do so. Imagine if such knowledge of others were applied above all to yourself. Wow! Stop for a moment at the end of this chapter and paint a picture of your strengths and weaknesses. Ask yourself if it is more important to blame yourself for your weaknesses or take advantage of your strengths. What if your strengths came together with your natural gifts? *Guaranteed success!*

What are your strengths? Your gifts? They are what you should spend your time on because you cannot have all the skills in a lifetime. If you are obsessed with perfection and mastering all the knowledge you think is important, here's a secret: You might not have talent or a gift in a particular field, but there is nothing that beats hard work. While people sleep, you work; while people listen to the news, you acquire new skills; while people underestimate you, you work behind the scenes. And one day, they will see a *new you*. There is nothing that continuous effort cannot overcome. If this is your situation, no excuse justifies someone in your field working harder than you. I am not the most gifted person in the world or in my field or in my time—far from it—but I have relied on my strengths and hard work. Have I succeeded? No, I'm still working on it. Can I do better? Yes. And you? Where are you in this process? Do you think you're the best? There is always someone who is going to break your record someday, but you can decide to be the man or woman of the moment.

Your Network of Contacts: An Immense Wealth

You can have *financial security*, thanks to what you know, but you become *financially independent*, thanks to whom you know; you certainly achieve *financial freedom*, thanks to your influence on your network of contacts. Your network of contacts is your collective brain, which works for you and with you. With it, you are not on your own: It completes and expands your possibilities without you having to master everything. Learning a profession and a skill is good, but getting to know those around you, wherever they are from, is the beginning of an endless fortune, which, when properly used, can change your life forever and reverberate across generations. Learning to acquire knowledge through learning is good, but you should get to know yourself and the potential of people around you wherever they are from.

The Ladder of Success

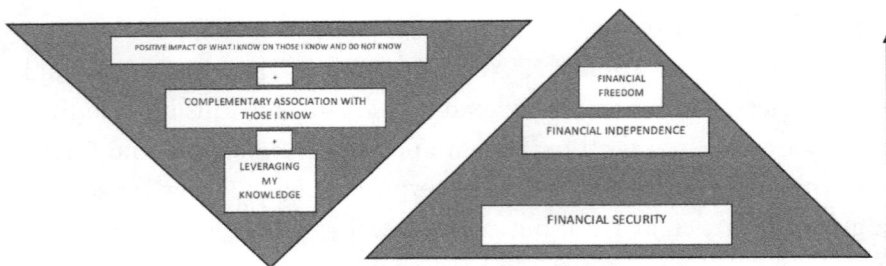

The Magic Cloud

The concept of the magic cloud encourages and spurs on people who want to succeed in paying more attention to everything around them. It encourages you to create a network of contacts around you because you never know how or when it can be useful in life. The concept is based on the theory that people who are employees are focused on their own concerns. They are basically in a box and stay within the system. Men and women aspiring to become entrepreneurs achieve self-fulfillment and become wealthy by paying attention to the people around them. They are alert and attentive to everyone's personal life and actions. They know that, sooner or later, the customers, associates, or suppliers they meet could become useful or have a direct or indirect strategic influence on their target market.

It is a multistage concept:

1. **Becoming aware**: As an entrepreneur or project developer, manager, or business executive, you take initiatives and actions, observe, and think over the long term in a way that goes beyond your understanding and ability to see. You must be original, authentic, and above all, attentive to everything around you because those around you play a major role in your success, and you must never forget it.

2. **Openness**: Staying open to others ensures that they remain open to you. People tend to react to you based on how you act toward them. This openness is broader in the sense that it requires an acceptance of others and their cultures and different ways of thinking as well as cooperation with the people who make up your immediate environment or its outskirts. This must be understood and accepted.

3. **Identifying key people**: They are the ones who share part of your private life; you know one another well enough to have things in common. They influence the people you want to reach who live outside your circle. They allow you to expand your circle of friends, customers, associates, and suppliers through references, which is and remains a better way to reach a given target faster without resorting to a burdensome approach.

4. **Contact management and development**: You need to explore, conquer, retain, and satisfy your entire circle of contacts if you want to benefit from them one day. This will leverage your impact and expand your database, which diversifies your customers, work team, suppliers, and partners. You should note that in this context prospecting means building bonds by getting to know others and maintaining your circle of friends and contacts to get the most out of it. This may require time and specific techniques for approaching them.

This process is a way to acquire a market share without spending significant sums of money. No matter what sector you want to go into, putting it into practice will give you a nice base and balance in the medium and long terms.

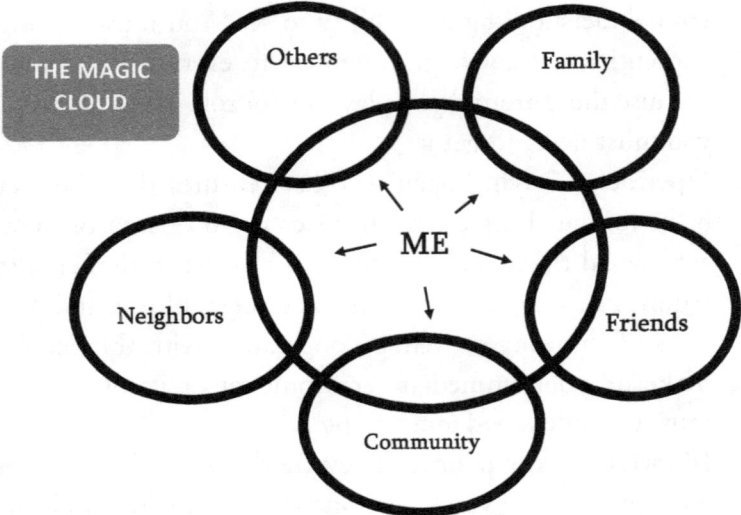

Take the example of someone who is thinking about opening a restaurant. As soon as she has written her business plan, she should already realize that the success of the project depends on her actions and response to the direct and indirect environment, which is likely to have an impact on the company she is building. Therefore, she adjusts her attitude toward external but non-negligible factors surrounding her, and she informs herself about mindsets, eating habits, traditions, the competition, the local population, and so on. She responds by working to meet the needs in her environment and, above all, by improving the quality of service as much as she can. She must then identify the people who influence business in the sector, approach them, get to know them, and work with them for medium- and long-term expansion.

The last step is to keep everything in a database: contacts, references, important information, statistics, dates, and events. This allows better management and business development. However, it should be noted that the approach may vary in complexity, depending on the sector, size, and current socioeconomic circumstances. Nevertheless, the steps are the same and will stay that way; no special knowledge of economics and business management is needed to be successful. The magic cloud is an asset: Learn about it, understand it, and put it into practice as much as possible if you seek a positive response from your market and network.

You have just taken a *step*: progress focused on success.

TO REMEMBER

CHAPTER 1

YOU CAN HAVE *financial security*, thanks to what you know, but you become *financially independent*, thanks to whom you know; you certainly achieve *financial freedom*, thanks to your influence on your network of contacts. Your network of contacts is your collective brain, which works for you and with you.

THE LAW OF A POSITIVE ATTITUDE

Your attitude, not your aptitude,
will determine your altitude.
—Zig Ziglar

Attitude: An Invincible Weapon

AN EVEN FASTER way to get to the top is mastering your *attitude*. A positive attitude overcomes all rules and life obstacles. The lion is the *king* of the forest, certainly not because of his height, weight, or intelligence, but because of his *attitude*. Knowledge mastered in your professional field is essential, but a *positive attitude* can make you the *king* of your environment, field, and time. As Zig Ziglar says, "Your attitude, not your aptitude, will determine your altitude." What is your attitude toward the various everyday circumstances in your life? On a sheet of paper, write down your general attitude and ask yourself if it is the desired attitude that will take you to the top. If the answer is yes, then what would you say to elevating it to an even higher level and having an impact on more men and women who are eager for achievement and success? If your answer is no, then this chapter will guide you to adopting the attitude of a norm-disrupting winner.

Faith as an Ally of Your Attitude

From 2006 to 2013, life battered me from all directions. I was trying to understand the business world, and my business was floundering. For seven years, I looked for ways to carry out my business plans; the main obstacle that I always came up against was financial. Over time, I realized that I did not know anyone who could help me, really listen to me, and believe in me. I searched, hit the pavement, knocked on the doors of banks, and wrote to sell projects that seemed lucrative both for me and potential investors. Alas, I didn't know anyone; moreover, I was a nobody. However, I never gave up. I always kept the flame burning within me: I maintained an attitude of trust and faith in God and the future. Anyway, that was all I had left. I thought about my mother who, when I was three years old, would knock on every door to sell her merchandise without losing hope. If she didn't do so, the next few days would be bleak for my brothers and me. What made her so motivated, so brave, so persevering? What made Thomas Edison so persistent in his experiments? It is the same thing that manages to keep me brave, smiling, confident, and enthusiastic: a positive attitude combined with my faith in God.

A positive attitude can make you unshakeable. Even the worst situation in the world cannot challenge a positive attitude; it forever changes the way you perceive what is happening to you and improves your response to adversity. Your strategy should always be to look for and find the solution behind any problem and not dwell on the problem itself. If the world moves forward because of inventions, if technology continues to create wonders in this world, it is because there are men and women who decide to be the solution. Your positive attitude helps in every earthly victory. That is something that successful men and women have in common. The question you need to ask is, how can you develop a positive attitude?

Knowing Your Motivations

In my case, I knew throughout my difficulties that I came from an impoverished family. I wasn't born with a silver spoon in my mouth. Nobody knew who we were, and we didn't know anyone important. I was aware that no one, except my mother, cared about my daily tribulations or even my plans.

Having an awareness of who I was and where I came from was primordial. If I gave up, no one would come to my rescue. If I wanted to see my plans come to fruition, I had to walk with my head high and show strength in all circumstances. In other words, you must dig deep into yourself to know your motivations and your why. If they do not make you cry, they are not strong enough. They might not make me cry, but they should make you cry.

Developing Positive Thinking

You need to cultivate positive thoughts that will nourish your *why* and always keep the flame burning. You must believe more than anyone that you will achieve your ends, regardless of the circumstances in your life. You can meet life's challenges because life is what it is, but you can decide how you live it. These positive thoughts nourish your mind and should remain active there every day. Cultivating habits that nurture your positive attitude in everyday life is a huge asset and a strategy that will make you an exceptional, formidable person. What adjectives would you use to describe yourself? Jot them down on a sheet of paper and meditate on them. Compare these adjectives with those you identify with your everyday heroes who have succeeded in their lives. Be honest with yourself; otherwise, seek the help of a relative, loved one, or stranger who can give an objective, constructive viewpoint. Change, if necessary, by adopting different habits in your daily life and a better attitude. The process may be long, but it is worth it.

Choose a lifestyle that matches your aspirations and thoughts and that leads you toward self-improvement. Dissociate yourself from mediocrity and seek excellence at all times. Accompany your thoughts with *actions* that back them up.

To develop and maintain a positive attitude, you also need to do the following:

1. Know your *why*: Why do you do what you do? What does this project mean to you?
2. Cultivate and develop positive thoughts every day to enhance your attitude.
3. Undertake *actions* in line with your thoughts and keep at it.
4. Learn from your *mistakes* and *failures*; they are rich in teachings.
5. Spend time with, listen to, and read about people who think and live like you, are going where you want to go, or are already there.

Adversity Reveals Your True Identity

The expected results may change from day to day and year to year, but your positive attitude should never change. Your attitude is, in other words, a part of your identity.

How would you describe how you respond to adversity? How will you act on the day your business is suffering huge losses? What will your reaction be when you lose a loved one? How will you react to the announcement of a refusal to fund your project despite many hours of work? How will you respond to any of life's setbacks? Describe the scenario on a blank sheet, close your eyes for a moment, and then open them after reflecting in a dark, quiet atmosphere. If, after a few minutes of meditation and reflection, immediate solutions and lessons learned do not become clear in your mind, then you are far from success. Ideally, you ask yourself what you missed—what's the problem? Learn more so that you are always maturing. The one and only way to fully pass this life test is to always maintain a positive attitude in all life circumstances, whether they be significant or trifling, economic or social, physical or emotional.

Activities

A. List five different negative reactions you experience when an unexpected situation arises and disrupts your plans:

1. ....
2. ....
3. ....
4. ....
5. ....

B. Now find five opposing reactions to the previous ones, which focus on keeping your cool and finding solutions:

1. ....
2. ....
3. ....

BLAISE NZETCHOANG N.

4. ....

5. ....

Reflection

If for A, you easily completed the five points without much hesitation in three minutes, you must absolutely adjust your attitude to new immediate reactions to unforeseen events and adversity if you yearn to achieve success.

If for B, you managed to complete the five points with difficulty or failed to complete them, you might react like a victim in some situations. Find a quick method for seeking solutions that aims to get you out of this mind state and makes you more accountable.

Consider this: Every problem you face in everyday life hides a solution just waiting to be found and which, in my opinion, could put you a few months or even years ahead of other people. And even if you don't yet see it, note that a piece of knowledge is a solution to a problem that has not yet been encountered.

You miss out on financial success, the love of your life, glory, and even victory because of your reaction to life circumstances and your attitude about what happens to you. Everything that happens to you contains a message that you need to grasp to move forward and improve. Are you receptive to the message? Is your attitude conducive to achieving personal growth in the situation? This law is so important to success that it will not change tomorrow or in the next decade or more. The only thing to do is to master it as soon as you can. If you are reading this book, you are traveling down the right road—the road to success.

You have just taken a *step*: progress focused on success.

CHAPTER 2

A POSITIVE ATTITUDE CAN make you unshakeable. Even the worst situation in the world cannot challenge a positive attitude; it forever changes the way you perceive what is happening to you and improves your response to adversity. Your strategy should always be to look for and find the solution behind any problem and not dwell on the problem itself. If the world moves forward because of inventions, if technology continues to create wonders in this world, it is because there are men and women who decide to be the solution. Your positive attitude helps in every earthly victory. That is something that successful men and women have in common. The question you need to ask is, how can you develop a positive attitude?

PATIENCE AND PERSEVERANCE

P ATIENCE IS A recognized trait among wealthy people in general; those who do not practice it will remain poor for the rest of their lives. Many people undertake wonderful things, do wonderful work in different fields, but very few succeed because they are not patient or not patient enough. Every success has its roots in the patience of those who seek it.

Experience Is an Asset

Desire without knowledge is not good,
and whoever makes haste with his feet misses his way.
—Proverbs 19:2

In 2009, I was part of the leadership of the company CAC SARL. I worked on many projects and partnerships, but I often missed my chance because I wasn't patient and informed enough. Patience was a quality I lacked. But I was doing great things and was very enthusiastic. If only I had learned the patience the business world requires, I would have already made a fortune. Yet I might not have had the inspiration to write this book to help you succeed better by learning from my mistakes.

Successful people are inspired by those who have succeeded, but to make your success happen sooner, learn from the mistakes of those who have failed repeatedly in their career. When you are convinced that you are on the right track with a business or business development project, it is, of course, important to proactively create success, but you must wait for the work and investment to come to fruition. Nowadays, many entrepreneurs, especially young people, make the mistake of wanting quick results. They recruit personnel and realize after a few days or weeks that the results are not materializing; they change tactics thinking there is a problem. I recommend patience if personnel demonstrate a willingness to learn. Time must be taken to train employees and allow training to bear fruit. Constant staff turnover is an enormous expense for companies hoping to magically find the right person for a job or task. Wanting immediate results creates negative pressure, especially if the preparation has not been done and plans are not well developed.

Wealth Comes to Those Who Wait

> Wealth gained hastily will dwindle,
> but whoever gathers little by little will increase it.
> —Proverbs 13:11

I am going to tell you John's story. He started from nothing to become the most important person at a giant in the mining industry. John has been an orphan since his early youth. He was a studious, ambitious boy, but he was tormented by his life circumstances. He had average intelligence but was hardworking and endowed with an unparalleled willingness to learn. John lived with an uncle who took him in after his parents died from illness. John was taking his last class before university studies, but he was so troubled in those difficult times that he had to retake the class three times. His uncle, impatient and concerned about the costs of John's education and under pressure from his wife, asked him to leave home to work in the mines.

John left home desperate and despondent and took refuge in a friend's house. From his friend's home, he sought work in a company a few kilometers away. His interview lasted only one minute because candidates were judged in action, not by the quality of their résumés. John worked so hard that the foreman noticed him and gave him the task of supervising the other employees. John was reliable and detail-oriented—a model employee. He acted diligently and respectfully; he was selected by a senior human resources officer to benefit from an internal program aimed at identifying employees who could represent the future of the publicly traded company. The program was designed to enable them to continue their studies and eventually specialize in various fields. John was able to continue his studies, receive a university education, and become an engineer. He spent all his vacations with the company and conquered the hearts of all the high-ranking personnel. He managed to save enough money to buy shares in the company. When he completed his studies and obtained a permanent contract in the company's management, he, nevertheless, maintained a modest lifestyle. All his money was reinvested in the company's pension fund because he believed in its future. In fact, the company highly valued its personnel and gave them an important place in their order of priorities.

One day, at an executive meeting, John was invited to defend a project. He was modestly dressed, unlike everyone else in the room, and attracted the attention of the CEO. At the end of the meeting, the CEO asked to speak with him privately. After some discussion, the manager realized that the young man had invested more than 80 percent of his income over the last five years in company shares—a sum of more than $200,000. Impressed by such a gesture, he asked him why he was doing that. He replied that the company believed in him, invested in him, that it was patient, and had, thereby, contributed to making him who he is today. He believed that such a business had a future and that it was wise for him to invest in it. The CEO appreciated the praise of the company, and he regularly wanted to speak with him because he liked to hear his thoughts. A few years later, the old man entrusted the management of the business to John before he died. Two years later, John had doubled the company's profits. His uncle, who was once impatient and anxious for a short-term return on investment, felt remorse and asked his nephew for forgiveness, admitting that he was a great source of inspiration for him.

Patience is a powerful weapon that can raise you to the height of your ambitions. Cultivating it is like mastering the cycle of growing corn. Every step is important, and no matter what the obstacles are, you must be patient, or someone else will benefit from the fruit of your labors.

John worked hard during those years. He was not just patient; he was persevering. Patience alone is not enough; you must wait and do the right thing over and over and over again, hoping that one day you will reap the bounty. Take the example of an athlete who trains for many years, sometimes a lifetime, to experience glory five, ten, or fifteen years later. If he had stopped improving, what would he have achieved? Patience and perseverance are essential if you want to be successful in what you do. A continuous effort is needed to rise to the top of your art or to the heights of success. No one can feel the pain more than you, but only you experience pride when you come to the end of your work and reach the top. People who say *no* to your opportunity, your application, or your project should give you a reason to continue to tirelessly excel. They harden you. They contribute directly or indirectly to the person you will be. They make you even better than yesterday's version of you. Learn to control your thoughts when such adversity faces you. Cultivate patience but stay in the action and keep working hard if you want to be successful in your businesses.

Discipline Helps Achieve Success

Persevering is good, but no one really manages to do so without a constant struggle against themselves, without instilling a permanent discipline that tames their undisciplined nature. No one is born disciplined. I will admit that. However, you can undoubtedly become disciplined. Discipline is learned, developed, and improved over time if you seek to progress. Humans are naturally undisciplined, and in the absence of rules and control, they plunge into anarchy like wild animals. For an individual to be more productive, one must uphold personal discipline, which, as you probably already know, is not easy to do. People who practice self-discipline successfully are one step ahead and are apt to achieve their *goal* in life much faster—even if they are less gifted than others who, on the other hand, are quite gifted but undisciplined. For me, discipline is to the disease of procrastination what Doliprane is to headaches: a cure. Discipline is a rare trait found in wealthy people.

BLAISE NZETCHOANG N.

Ronald and Christian were two professional soccer players who played internationally. Ronald was highly gifted to the extent that it seemed that he was born with a ball on his foot. He knew how to handle the ball and had fun on a soccer field like no one else could. But Ronald was always out partying before important games. He came late for practices and failed to meet his professional commitments. Although beloved by all, his lack of discipline had a negative impact on the team's cohesiveness and the pursuit of their collective goal; as a result, his professional career lasted only seven years. On the other hand, Christian was less talented than Ronald but was unparalleled in his profession. He never missed practices and always showed up an hour ahead of time; furthermore, he never drank alcohol in the seventy-two hours before a game, followed instructions to the letter, and listened to everyone. Everyone listened to him, and he was always taken very seriously on the team. He always said, "I play soccer as a surgeon performs an operation. The slightest mistake can be fatal to the patient." Christian became the captain of almost every team he played for and played more than fifteen years in the professional league. His discipline earned him exceptional awards, cups, magazine covers, and millions of dollars in salary and advertising revenues.

Activity

On a scale of one (not at all) to ten (completely), rate how disciplined you are at work, at home, in your projects, at school, or in your resolutions.

Answer:

List the ten most important things that prevent you from being disciplined in your everyday activities.

1. ....
2. ....
3. ....

4. ....
5. ....
6. ....
7. ....
8. ....
9. ....
10. ....

If you have ten, you have the wrong people around you and are on the wrong path.

Now resolve to fulfill your obligations and honor the commitments you make to yourself and others. Put this resolution on paper.

Resolution:

....
....
....

Read this resolution aloud every morning and evening and, if possible, ask someone to follow up with you about it. Set a weekly meeting date to track and evaluate your progress for at least three months. A weekly schedule will certainly help you with this task.

Witness/mentor: ....
Day of follow-up: ....
Time of follow-up: ....
Comments: ....

Time Optimization

Effective time management is an important factor in success. Michael Jordan had only twenty-four hours a day when he was still playing basketball, yet he was able to practice much more than his contemporaries. The same could be said of Theodore Roosevelt, Henry Ford, and Andrew Carnegie, who also left their mark on their era with remarkable political and economic achievements. Were they superheroes? Aliens or superhuman? No. You must apply the rules and principles that lead to success. What they entail was indispensable yesterday to anyone who wanted to be successful; they still are today and will be tomorrow.

One of the things that helps make successful men superhuman is undoubtedly their ability to effectively manage their days. Discipline reflects efficient time management. Planning days or even weeks ahead and having some core routine activities help keep your life running smoothly. Doing everything in its time, focusing on what you enjoy and do well, delegating when necessary—many tasks can propel you to success.

Activity

1. Do you feel at loose ends some days? Prepare an efficient weekly schedule and fill in the gaps based on your plans.
2. Do you feel that you are not enjoying your business? Change careers.
3. Do you feel like you are doing too much? Review your priorities.
4. Do you feel like you are playing it by ear? Set yourself a clear, concise *goal*; a clear, concise agenda will help you achieve it with small daily objectives.
5. Go over each day and reward yourself when you have done what you had planned to do. Take it one day at a time, and you will undoubtedly succeed.

If, in my twenties, *patience and perseverance* had been on my side, I might have become a multimillionaire before I was twenty-five years old. Mastering these traits can give you control over your destiny. It's up to you; you can start today and witness the change. If you decide to begin today, you are on the way to success.

You have just taken a *step*: progress focused on success.

CHAPTER 3

ONE DAY, AT an executive meeting, John was invited to defend a project. He was modestly dressed, unlike everyone else in the room, and attracted the attention of the CEO. At the end of the meeting, the CEO asked to speak with him privately. After some discussion, the manager realized that the young man had invested more than 80 percent of his income over the last five years in company shares—a sum of more than $200,000. Impressed by such a gesture, he asked him why he was doing that. He replied that the company believed in him, invested in him, that it was patient, and had, thereby, contributed to making him who he is today. He believed that such a business had a future and that it was wise for him to invest in it. The CEO appreciated the praise of the company, and he regularly wanted to speak with him because he liked to hear his thoughts. A few years later, the old man entrusted the management of the business to John before he died. Two years later, John had doubled the company's profits.

4

THE LAW OF LOVE

S UCCESS WITHOUT INTEGRITY is nothing just as success without love will not last. In this chapter, we discuss the role of *love* as an ingredient of true, infallible, eternal *success*.

It is written in the book of Ephesians 3:17–19, "I pray that you may have your roots and foundation in love, so that you, together with all God's people, may be CAPABLE of understanding how broad and long, how high and deep, is Christ's love." Ignorance made me suffer for many years. More important, my selfish love caused many people who loved me to suffer. You can easily get carried away by the desire to succeed in your projects to the point of missing out on what is essential in life: *love*. Yes, be careful not to hurt those who love you unconditionally. Success is good, but do not let yearning for success rob you of your humanity, make you insensitive, or blind you to the point of having a stone heart instead of a live, beating heart.

Of course, you should fervently seek the roads to success, but giving your life meaning is crucial. The success we aspire for is only earthly, and we will be called to account during the Last Judgment. You can succeed by pursuing your projects differently: out of love and with love for yourself, others, and God. Beyond your socioeconomic success, how do you want to be remembered after your life on earth? We all will have to be accountable one day. We will not bring anything with us; therefore, you should imbue your success with a deeper meaning. Whoever you are, if you hurt people on your path to success, I recommend that you go over your priorities and put the good that your initiative will cause first instead of what you will gain from it. For soldiers of the Christian faith, or for those who are curious to learn more, I recommend the Bible.

It says in 1 Peter 1:17–18, "And if you call on him as Father who judges impartially according to each one's deeds, conduct yourselves with fear throughout the time of your exile, knowing that you were ransomed from the futile ways inherited from your forefathers, not with perishable things such as silver or gold, but with the precious blood of Christ, like that of a lamb without blemish or spot."

Doing Business but Doing It Differently

It is time to go back to the basics and give meaning to your story by loving your neighbor as yourself with your works on earth. Make your achievements an eternal *success*.

Imagine the originality of your project, your company, or your work in light of the love it brings to all stakeholders. Just imagining it is beautiful. What if you make the dream *come true*?

Love is a positive, selfless feeling toward a person or group of people. Without love, we are nothing but worthless wrapping paper, and everything we do is devoid of feeling and, therefore, empty. Without love, man is mechanical, numb to what surrounds him, and his endeavours are without real impact and devoid of divine blessing. The only things that make you live on forever on this earth are your works that have touched and continue to touch people even after you are gone; it is the love that you have given to the world through your being, works, or actions.

Love is the difference between success and eternal success. I recommend that you seek eternal success. *Love* can make you creative, innovative, and above all, eternal.

Because this book aims to develop business skills, we will discuss self-love, love of those close to you, love for your work team, love for your company, love for your clients, and above all, the love that surpasses any other, the love of God. Love as described here is an asset in any initiative aimed at success and wealth. Your financial success depends, among other things, on the love that flows within and between the five circles that I call the magic circles of success.

The magic circles are the result of reflections in recent years that have allowed me to see beyond my mere self and understand that my success alone was not enough. I had to create a balance between myself, my family, my associates or colleagues, my clients, my company, and God the Father. This balance ensures long-term success and brings value to your products and services.

Many people do not know how to appreciate the grace bestowed upon them by the everlasting leader of leaders that makes them so powerful and so likely to achieve the impossible.

Reflection on the Holy Scriptures at the beginning of my work led me to question Pastor Stéphane Gagné of the Église Baptiste Évangélique Vie nouvelle in Joliette. His work was a tremendous help for the depths of the following analysis of love.

Love of God and a Business's Economic Situation

God's love is the first love that invariably guides the love of others—of colleagues, employers, customers, and yourself. His essence is love. He was the first to love. The school of love is in God through His Son Jesus Christ, who gave Himself to the cross to pay the debt of our sins, trespasses, and offenses.

If I love God, I will want to admire Him.

We often feel affection and admiration for people we venerate in sports, media, or business. Yet God is an entrepreneur. He created the universe, and He knows how it works. The first thing that is revealed to us about God in the Bible is that He works, acts, and shapes: "In the beginning, God created the heavens and the earth."

If I love God, I will want to imitate Him.

No one has ever undertaken anything more important and grandiose than creating the whole universe. Amazing capabilities are required to accomplish these things. That is why He is worthy of worship and praise. We must recognize His skill, authority, and wisdom.

If I love God, I will want to listen to Him.

In the Bible, God deploys all His wisdom—spiritual and legislative (laws, rules, ordinances), community-related (wealth management, wills, property), ethical (good, evil, guilt), and practical.

If I love God, I will want to respect Him.

Everything belongs to God, and He wants to share everything. God wants to bless us so that we can bless others in turn. My management of assets and resources reveals my heart, intentions, and values. We will have to account not only for everything we have said, done, and thought but also for how we have managed what God has lent us, including the financial resources, the opportunities to do what is right, and the way we have treated our employees and even our customers (James 5).

If I love God, I will want to adore Him.

Everything exists for God. Everything exists through God. Everything glorifies God. Your companies, family, actions, and leisure activities are part of this plan. It is wise to attune everything you do with everything He has done, what He does, and what He will do. To rally to His plans through His word is a guarantee of success. A few years ago, R. G. Letourneau, founder of the famous Caterpillar heavy machinery company, fully devoted his company to God's glory. He managed his business by applying the eternal principles God gives in His word. He has thus enjoyed financial success while honoring the One from whom all things come.

To love God is to enter into His plans. It is to trust Him and believe in His skill, words, and good and holy intentions.

The Love That Leads You to a New Way of Doing Business

God's love gives the proper perspective on what is truly important in life. The creation was made in a relational framework. The reason the universe exists is God's wish to enter into free communion with His creatures. God unfolds all His love through the beauty, immensity, and perfection of His creation. The fruit of His labor is an expression of His affection for us.

As Jesus says, "So whatever you wish that others would do to you, do also to them" (Matthew 7:12). If this gospel truth were applied in companies, the quality of production would be greatly improved. Unfortunately, we want to receive the best and give in the most lackluster way. Selfishness hinders business development—selfishness, jealousy, and rivalries. If we acted out of love for others and according to one another's gifts, not according to convention or seniority but by placing the best person for the task at the time, we would achieve much different results.

Love of God changes a person. It changes your heart, motivations, ambitions, and conduct. If the company exists only by me and for me, it reflects the cancer of our society: selfishness. But if it is through us and for us, it serves the interests of humanity and will do much good for our needy world.

Proportionality, according to the apostle Paul, is a rule of social equity in which the rich, the wealthiest, and the most educated take care of the poorest, the indigent, and apprentices. The Bible suggests that you use your abundance to help your poor neighbors (2 Corinthians 8:13-14). When people understand that their blessings are given to bless others, their work is part of a real transformation of our society.

Your understanding of work will change. Work is a blessing that God bestows on man. That has been His wish since the beginning of humankind. Your job does not define you, and your salary does not define your identity. Therefore, you can experience joy at work by understanding that it is a chance to thrive by using your gifts, an opportunity to do good to those who receive your services, and a privilege to glorify God through the work of your hands.

The quality of your work often depends on a sound understanding of whom you serve: Serving the queen or serving a simple citizen is not done exactly the same way or with the same thoroughness. Yet in the Bible, Christians are called to serve their masters as if they were serving Christ himself. In fact, the principle is that the person before you does not matter because, ultimately, you serve the Lord. This means you are liberated from scrutinizing people before you. Conversely, when you practice favoritism based on class, race, and education, it skews your performance, quality, and service.

The love of God leads you to submit yourself to the authorities and established rules (Romans 13). You are not free to change or modify the frameworks established by supervisors. Doing this leads to disruption and chaos. God invites us to please the one who hired us and those who will benefit from our services. This attitude changes your relationship with your employer and partners and makes you an honest, upright, respectful businessperson—and not just in front of the supervisor or customer. No tricks, no schemes (Colossians 3:22–25).

Man is called to work wholeheartedly and use all his effort and talents to serve others. Half-hearted effort gets you halfway to where you want to go but doubles the exasperation and frustration of your product's consumers. The principle of reaping what has been sown applies not only to agriculture but also to all spheres of secular and spiritual life (Galatians 6:7).

You work hoping that the best lies ahead. Yes, the best is to come. There is a reward after this life here on earth for those who are faithful and who put into practice the wise principles given by God (Colossians 3:24).

A Love That Renews You Every Day

In the Bible, greatness is revealed by the ability to serve others in good and bad times. Humility is a mark of great maturity in a person because it means that you do not depend on others for your sense of worth. Your dignity and importance do not lie in what you possess or in your position but in your relationships; if you know that you are loved from above, you will not rely on others when choosing your actions, however small they may be. In fact, Jesus tells us that faithfulness in small things is a sign of maturity that will attract greater responsibilities later.

Self-Esteem and Self-Worth

Loving yourself is the beginning of a happy life. Giving yourself love and respect and recognizing your own worth is the very basis for all success. How can you achieve great things if you lack self-esteem? Learn to love yourself as you are. Life goes on and will continue to do so after you, but you can decide to live proudly by beginning a process of acceptance and respect for yourself. Your life is short and a perpetual struggle that sometimes makes your existence quite painful. In your life, you owe it to yourself to love yourself as you are and improve yourself to more fully appreciate who you are. Giving yourself what you want is a way to show your self-love without becoming a compulsive shopper. No one will do it for you. Deciding to be happy is an important step in the process leading to success. Making this decision and following up with concrete actions is a sign of the love you have for yourself.

Why do a job you do not like? Why work with people you do not enjoy? Is it for money? If so, what is the point of having so much money if that money or the way you earn it does not make you happy? Loving yourself means making decisions, first and foremost, for yourself; if you are not in harmony with yourself, you will not be in harmony with others or your environment.

Group versus Team

Many people can work together without being on the same team. Being part of the same team requires having a common vision and purpose and respecting one another while paying no heed to origin, culture, and differences. For superior performance and strong cohesiveness, you must respect and love those fighting alongside you, whether they are your colleagues, associates, supervisors, or subordinates. If you feel obliged to work with people you do not like, friction will probably arise between you, and the group will be unproductive. You must be part of a group of people you love and enjoy working with every day. This will lead everyone to do their part, creating a collective individualism where everyone gives it their best, without comparisons or cheating for better results. Loving your coworkers helps create team spirit, healthy competition, loyalty to one another, creativity, and an ability to go beyond barriers and limits. That inevitably contributes to forming a winning *team*.

The company as a corporate entity is nothing without those who comprise it. It must be loved by these people. Without them, the company would not exist. As business leaders or managers, we need to create an environment conducive to the development of employees or associates, which could encourage their dedication. Human beings must be at the center of your business because of your love for them. Loving your employees and associates can help earn their loyalty, which could be something like a love for the company itself.

A connection with the company's mission, values, products, and services justifies fully loving it. Stakeholders bound by such a feeling guarantee a healthy, sustainable collaboration. You need to work in a company you love if you want to get the most out of the time you spend there. Financial gain alone does not justify devoting your entire life to serving a company. You should love it for its cause and societal orientations.

1. How does your company affect society?
2. Does it have a human side?
3. Are customers satisfied with it? Are they exploited or assisted?
4. If you were a customer, would you be satisfied?
5. Are you in the right place for you? Are you respected at your fair value?
6. Can you help improve things?

These are some ideas that should guide your decisions about the love you give your company and the love you expect from it. With such an asset, the company could rise to the top.

Loving Your Customers Could Guarantee Their Loyalty

Customers ask for nothing more than to be satisfied with what they pay for. You must love them for the decision to do business with you. You need to work to maintain and improve the relationship and build loyalty. Loving your customers requires always being better to satisfy them, innovating to keep them, informing and communicating to demonstrate your attachment to them, and above all, sharing your vision and actions for the community. Loving your customers means giving more than what they pay for. If a customer stays or comes back, he or she loves you; there's nothing more to it than that. And that's what it takes for it to be reciprocal. It is often said the customer is *king*, but it is your thoughtfulness that honors their royalty and gives the saying its real meaning. It is nothing but gratitude to those who trust you through a commitment to what you are offering them.

You must respond to this commitment with gestures of gratitude. Anyone who participates directly or indirectly in your business's success deserves recognition, respect, and gratitude from you.

Activities

1. Develop a charter or a code of ethics that aims to set rules of conduct for everyone.
2. Offer a smile and gratitude to all those who are directly or indirectly involved in your project or company.
3. Invest in community development.
4. Give and do more than what customers, employees, and partners expect of you.
5. A sincere *thank you* is enough. Always finish with a *big* smile.

Love is a feeling that drives you to do the impossible for a better world that is a good place to live. Incorporating it into your everyday activities shelters you from need and protects you from an unhappy life. It all starts with love for and of God, self-esteem, love of your family, and love of the stakeholders in your business. Anyone who makes that a priority in their business principles and everyday work is guaranteed ineluctable, eternal success.

You have just taken a *step*: progress focused on success.

CHAPTER 4

A S JESUS SAYS, "So whatever you wish that others would do to you, do also to them" (Matthew 7:12). If this gospel truth were applied in companies, the quality of production would be greatly improved. Unfortunately, we want to receive the best and give in the most lackluster way. Selfishness hinders business development—selfishness, jealousy, and rivalries. If we acted out of love for others and according to one another's gifts, not according to convention or seniority but by placing the best person for the task at the time, we would achieve much different results.

5

THE LAW OF GOALS

*A life or business without a genuine, unique, specific goal
is similar to a journey without a specific destination.*

WHY DO YOU exist? Why are you on this earth, in this particular place of the world, in this specific situation reading this book? Shouldn't your existence have a meaning and a *goal*? Shouldn't your daily progress be toward a specific result? What difference does your existence make on this earth? What do you mean to your society? How do you contribute to a better world? What is your *goal*? If you do not yet have one, this book, and this chapter in particular, encourages you to find one. Once you have defined a goal that gives meaning to your life, your perception of the world will not be the same. Do so today while these thoughts are still fresh in your mind. You certainly have something that defines you and could be a blessing to anyone who encounters it.

Activity

On a piece of paper, write down the five things that define and characterize you, excluding everything you do that is directly related to your family:

1. ....
2. ....
3. ....
4. ....
5. ....

Identify five issues in the world that your intrinsic traits and values would solve:

1. ....
2. ....
3. ....
4. ....
5. ....

- Identify a high-quality trait and associated solution that you derive a non-monetary pleasure from sharing.
- Formulate a sentence that best summarizes what you can do with the above and that gives real meaning to your existence and whose impact goes beyond your family circle.
- Reread the sentence several times for consecutive days. Does it express who you are? If the answer is no, repeat the exercise several times until you figure out what resonates with you. If the answer is yes, make it a goal that you are ready to fight for.

Being devoted to achieving your goals every day is important; your daily actions help achieve our unique and timeless *goal*. It is easy, and even common, to see people confuse their objectives with their *goal*. An objective may vary from one situation to another, from one place to another, from one period to another, and even based on circumstances that are sometimes beyond your control. However, a *goal* does not consider any of that. Here are examples of goals: spreading the word of God, contributing to the technological industry's development, and being an inspiring leader.

Defining a Clear, Concise Goal

The life goal of my wife *Tatiana* is to have a name that will precede her wherever she goes. Yes, she wants to make a fortune. She wants to achieve many things, but the most important thing for her is that people retain a positive memory of her actions—from the smallest to the most significant ones. She wants her children to be proud of the renown she gains for what she will have accomplished. She is as beautiful as an angel; she has a smile that leaves no one cold; she has a deep voice—she sounds like a rock singer. She is solid, upstanding, and reliable. She has a real smile and an attractive face that draws attention to her. But despite all that, that's not how she wants to be remembered. She wants to accomplish things and inspire and help those around her. She wants to be useful through her businesses. And that is how she would find fulfillment. That is her *goal* in life.

The *goal* of this book is to help you achieve success. Wealth is a *goal* that people very often want to achieve. But if it comes at the expense of those who are close to and around them, the *goal* runs counter to the seven eternal laws of success. Financial success must be the result of a *goal* that benefits the world. Many people refuse to talk about wealth because they only fight for themselves or not enough for others; they just exist. Whatever you do on earth, if you have a major impact that goes beyond your family circle or loved ones, wealth will inevitably ensue. This wealth will come in the form of wages, income, gifts, blessings, or in some other way, but it will come.

What is the difference between a small local retailer and an international retailer? What is the difference between a local motivational speaker and a motivational speaker who performs around the world? What is the difference between a local church and a congregation with thousands of people? If you find what makes the difference, you will find the secret of success. There is neither a small nor a large *goal*; there is only one *goal*. It is the greatness of the person behind the *goal* that makes all the difference.

Only Lazy People Disapprove of Wealth

Wealth comes to those who work day and night to achieve their *goal*. It is inevitable. I watched and listened to very wealthy people, and I found that they were people whose existence derived its meaning from and depended on what they wanted to accomplish and how they wanted the world to remember their existence.

I have cultivated the reflex of staying away from people who disapprove of wealth because *incompetence* often lies behind this way of thinking. The pursuit of wealth should not be a *goal* but a process that testifies to desire, determination, work, faith, investment, and patience in the pursuit of your *goal*. It's an odd concept for lazy people. Excuses characterize the lazy and ineluctably lead them to poverty. King Solomon was the richest person of all time and considered to be a man of preeminent wisdom. He wrote a collection of many teachings about wisdom. In Proverbs 24:33-34, it is written, "A little sleep, a little slumber, a little folding of the hands to rest, and poverty will come upon you like a robber, and want like an armed man."

Success Is a Process

Achieving success first requires a specific *goal*, fervent desire, years of reflection, work, patience, and some inevitable discomfort. The sooner you start, the sooner you are likely to achieve your ends. But one important thing to remember is that to succeed in this, you must stay focused and avoid the daily distractions that muddle your thoughts and waste your time.

If you yearn for financial wealth, you really need to define the amount of money you want to earn and meet some additional demands.

Activity

1. How much money do you want to earn?
2. By what date would you like to have it?
3. Do you know how to make it happen?
4. Are you forty years old or under?
5. Are you over forty?

Reflections

1. What if you aimed a little higher? *Vision.*
2. Do you need a game plan? Yes.
3. Are you employed? It will be difficult but not impossible. Are you in business? You can do it, but it will not be easy.
4. You may have the time but not the maturity. Look for a mentor.

5. You may have the maturity but not the time. Put more work into it.

Everyone with an entrepreneurial spirit has a much weightier *goal* than just the wish to make a fortune. A successful venture, first and foremost, requires inspiration, but making it happen requires effort.

Entrepreneurship Is 10 Percent Inspiration and 90 Percent Perspiration, But . . .

Another way to achieve financial independence is to go into business, buy a business, or even partner with people who are in business; not working for them, but with them. Entrepreneurship is 10 percent inspiration and 90 percent perspiration. However, over the short or medium term, you will enjoy the fruits of your labors. Although going into business is risky, I think you risk survival in this world if you do not do anything at all to improve your life. Yes, businesspeople are likely to suffer greater financial losses than everyone else. Don't panic. Take calculated risks, but take them because that is how you learn. You will probably fail somewhere, but you will gain invaluable wealth from what you learn in the process. Although failure is hard to take, it is a postponed success that reveals itself to the most persistent.

Doing business means accepting to do what 90 percent or 95 percent of people are not willing to do to attain what you attain. As a result, that means people whose *goal* is financial independence have a mindset that inevitably leads them to develop skills and maintain habits. If you want financial independence by a specific date, you will have it because simply yearning for it is proof that you have almost reached your destination.

You have just taken a *step*: progress focused on success.

TO REMEMBER

CHAPTER 5

WHY DO YOU exist? Why are you on this earth, in this particular place of the world, in this specific situation reading this book? Shouldn't your existence have a meaning and a *goal*? Shouldn't your daily progress be toward a specific result? What difference does your existence make on this earth? What do you mean to your society? How do you contribute to a better world? What is your *goal*? If you do not yet have one, this book, and this chapter in particular, encourages you to find one. Once you have defined a goal that gives meaning to your life, your perception of the world will not be the same. Do so today while these thoughts are still fresh in your mind. You certainly have something that defines you and could be a blessing to anyone who encounters it.

6

THE LAW OF FREEDOM

Do not lose your freedom!

F REEDOM IS A big concept: It refers to a person's or group's ability to act or move about. A free person is not a slave. But are you really free? More people than you think are captives. In Galatians 5:1, it is written, "For freedom Christ has set us free; stand firm therefore, and do not submit again to a yoke of slavery."

Examine your situation and get started making changes. Claim your identity and fight to be yourself and be free.

Avoiding Conformism

Look around you. Analyze your behavior and that of people around you; you will see that we are all or almost all acting under the influence of one another. That explains why so many people lack authenticity: They all want to be like everyone else in the masses for fear of being rejected. You believe otherwise, but this makes you a prisoner. The masses have never produced anything good. You must dissociate yourself from them as soon as possible and embrace projects that inspire you, even if they make you feel like you are going crazy. All genius has a touch of madness. Break free from the earthly captivity that leads you to die in poverty, ignorance, and want.

Avoiding Distraction Agents

Society is very influenced by what I call distraction agents, namely, television, the Internet, popular newspapers, and social media. These agents have a way of overdramatizing and creating a climate of panic and fear in the world. You should steer clear from them as much as possible if you cannot maturely sift through or manage the information they convey. None of these distraction agents know your personal life, past, ambitions, strengths, and weaknesses well enough to act objectively in your life, yet the information they spread sows panic that puts us on pins and needles. We follow them so closely that we miss out on everything that could give our lives meaning.

How many of us have ever thought of going into business? Completing a project? Surely many of us have done so, but have the people around you actively encouraged you to move forward with your project? Undoubtedly very few of them. Furthermore, if you socialize with people who do not have the same dreams as you or are not where you want to be, how many have the experience necessary to provide an objective opinion about your business plans? How can you gain experience in a venture if you don't go for it? Yes, your loved ones' opinions can be useful, but the opinion of experts in the field you are going into is better. Your loved ones can give you love, courage, and financial support but not objective advice on how to carry out your project, especially if they do not have any experience with that kind of venture.

Staying Free and Becoming the Master of Your Destiny

In my family, no one formally went into business before I did. Since I was young, I knew I needed to work for myself, no matter the price to pay; if I wanted to find fulfillment, I had to be my own boss. How? I had no idea how to go about it, but I needed to be trained, informed, and follow someone who was or had been successful. But above all, I needed enough failures to help me anticipate and avoid them as much as possible. Having grown up with and around brothers, sisters, relatives, close friends, and acquaintances who were employees, I quickly realized that this was not the way to go if I wanted to achieve my goals.

Learning to Follow Your Instincts

For several years in the beginning, I wallowed in debts, threats from creditors, unpaid rents, and sleepless nights. Nevertheless, an inner voice told me to stay the course and never give up—maybe change strategies, but never give up. I heeded that voice, which, despite the hardships, let me be me.

Almost no one around me understood me because my thinking was different from theirs. Do not try to be someone else just because people do not understand you or do not approve of your path or thinking. One of the best ways to fail in life and especially in business is to try to please, listen to, satisfy, and be there for everyone. You are the person who matters most. Listen to the voice inside you. Avoid believing that the logic that most people around you ascribe to is the best tool for success. Do you want to conform to norms that have currency with those around you who live an ordinary life and achieve ordinary things? Why not do things differently and make a difference by living according to the inner voice that challenges you to achieve the impossible? Yes, I understand the people who say going into business or starting a company is risky, but not taking any initiative to change your situation is even riskier. You must follow your instinct and rely on those who have achieved something like what you are trying to achieve. You can also simply call on professionals who can be your collective mind. The road has never been and still is not easy, but I know that trials and tribulations have made me a better person. I have simply followed my instinct.

Using the Concept of the Collective Mind

How many of us married someone out of conformism or to please our parents and society? How many of our loved ones have suffered the negative consequences of that union? Did that undertaking make you happy? If so, you are the exception. If not, it was predictable: You were under the influence of others. In other words, you were not free. The consequences of such subservience can destroy a life forever. The same goes for a company or project: You are the entrepreneur, the project developer; your ideas and ambitions carry a great deal of weight. You have only one life, and it is short. Whether you succeed or fail, it happens here in this life, so go big and go fast. Why not look for the ingredients, resources, and means that can increase your chances of success? Why not surround yourself with experts who have relevant technical knowledge?

Regardless of the opinion of those who are well informed or uninformed, your decision matters; otherwise, you would not be the project developer. Surround yourself with professionals, but keep in mind that you are the only decision-maker because it is your project and business.

Accept Being Different

For many years, I was considered a failure because I refused to conform to the way people around me did things. Although 99 percent or more of the people worked for someone, a company, or the government, I wanted to work for myself. That takes courage, let me tell you. It bothers others and can jeopardize the relationships with those around you, but do not give in because at some point, you need to be on your own to better understand who you are, what you want in life, and the direction you want to go. At that point, you will really see who believes in you.

Life gives you the best it has to offer if you know exactly what you expect from it. Fighting for your convictions without being influenced by public opinion is hard, but it is the only way to give your life meaning. You only have one life, and no matter the price to pay, you must live it your way and as if every day were your last, and that means living as a free man or woman. No one can be held accountable for your actions even if others have helped guide them; therefore, you must act and give your life meaning so that you leave your mark during your time on earth. Do not allow it to be the legacy that others want to leave through you. Be the protagonist of your life, business, or projects, and make sure you act to make the world a better place. Ask yourself, what if my company could make a difference? But to make a difference, you must act differently from others, not the way everyone wants you to act. At this stage of your reading, at this stage of the search for happiness, you are hungry for success. Remember that you feel that way because it is your calling.

Failure: The Great Teacher

For more than ten years, I learned from failure. It was my best teacher in entrepreneurship through many iterations of trial and error. But one of the things I promised myself was that I would never let others' opinions of me shape my reality. I endured mockery and bullying. I fought for my freedom every day. What people say or think about you can quickly become a cage you live in for the rest of your life if you let them get to you. Take a few minutes to think over your financial situation, and ask yourself whether you are where you want to be. Is your current situation the result of your own decisions? If, for a single moment, you do not like what you have or who you have become because of the others' influence, it is high time you changed the way you think, act, and above all, react to others and your environment. You might make mistakes, but you will gain priceless experience. Today's world was built by bold men and women. Failure, refusal, and rejection will only test your mettle: There is a tale to tell for every success.

Name five major failures or mistakes you have experienced in the last five years:

1. ....
2. ....
3. ....
4. ....
5. ....

List five resolutions or lessons you learned:

1. ....
2. ....
3. ....

4. ....

5. ....

Note: Repeating the same failures or mistakes would be an affront to your wisdom. Work harder and be on your way to success.

Examining Your Aspirations

A free person is not locked in a box or a single thought; he or she is not *confined to a job or an ideology*. Being free means being able to act without constraint and having an independence that allows you to act according to your beliefs and what you want, regardless of what others think. Fully commit to your projects and ideas. Believe in what you can achieve if you give it your all. Proudly strive for your *goals*, heedless of what others think and armed with expertise. Know that people who have never done anything great cannot be of great help to you. The road to success is not for those who are easily influenced and captives when it comes to their dreams and ideas. Entrepreneurs and leaders who have achieved great things and contributed to our society's development have shaken off rejections, loneliness, hardship, and ridicule: You must accept these hurdles. Taking advantage of adversity is the only way to go.

Avoiding Procrastination

Postponing what can be accomplished today until tomorrow is easy. That is what I call the disease of procrastination. You cannot imagine how many people suffer from this disease throughout the world. Having time, freedom, and decision-making authority can have far-reaching consequences for success. Many projects will never see the light of day because their developers are suffering from the disease of procrastination. Why am I talking about a disease? Because many people today suffer from this scourge. But the good news is that you can cure it. This chapter briefly provides remedies for this disease. It has devastating consequences in the lives of many people, and unfortunately, wasted time cannot be regained—but better late than never. Think of all the plans, work, and ideas that you have never taken a concrete action to bring to life. There are many symptoms of the disease, including fear, lack of discipline and self-confidence, incompetence, anxiety, lack of energy, and poor or non-existent time management. There are people around us who live in poverty. Others lose their jobs because of these symptoms. Many people are unaware of it. You need to know how to identify the symptoms of the disease of procrastination and cure them with immediate personal actions or the support of an expert in the matter who has mastered corrective measures.

It is time for the warrior within you to emerge and contribute, in one way or another, to creating a better world. You should quickly put these ideas into practice, assess the results, and adjust instead of letting others' fears and opinions smother your ambitions. It is up to you and you alone; if you do not do it, no one will do it for you.

Free yourself and take the plunge while the flame still shines bright.

You have just taken a *step*: progress focused on success.

TO REMEMBER

CHAPTER 6

Staying Free and Becoming the Master of Your Destiny

IN MY FAMILY, no one formally went into business before I did. Since I was young, I knew I needed to work for myself, no matter the price to pay; if I wanted to find fulfillment, I had to be my own boss. How? I had no idea how to go about it, but I needed to be trained, informed, and follow someone who was or had been successful. But above all, I needed enough failures to help me anticipate and avoid them as much as possible. Having grown up with and around brothers, sisters, relatives, close friends, and acquaintances who were employees, I quickly realized that this was not the way to go if I wanted to achieve my goals.

7

THE LAW OF ENERGY

Energy: A Wellspring of Happiness

S OME THINGS WILL help you forge ahead on your path to success. They are crucial if you want to fully enjoy that success. What is the point of a six-, seven-, or eight-digit account if you do not have the energy and strength to enjoy it while you are still alive? This chapter is critical to ensuring your success contributes, first and foremost, to your happiness and that of others. Yes, energy is an important factor in your well-being. Without it, your struggle will not last long and will not benefit your inheritors. It is an ingredient in remarkable performances, dynamism, endurance, and perseverance in your daily path. Generating growth in your business primarily requires the essential ingredients of personal growth and good health. The business world sometimes imposes a life without stoppages or breaks. It is often a frantic, relentless race for better business performance. Taking care of yourself has several advantages, and the energy you gain from doing so is contagious.

One thing an audience always remembers is a speaker's energy level. They do not always retain the speaker's words, but they will remember the energy he or she spoke with; it remains firmly etched in their minds. Energy, energy, and still more energy is the force behind momentum. Have you ever attended a show that made a real impression on you? What most captivated you?

Business leaders, executives, politicians, or anyone in an important position in an organization should take great care of their physical health, eat well, and engage in regular physical activity. Having an active, healthy sex life in your marriage, along with regular prayer, are recommended.

Healthy Eating

Hippocrates (460-370 BC) said, "Let thy food be thy medicine and medicine be thy food." I have noticed that the most important men and women in our society take excellent care of their health because their responsibilities require it.

Nutritionist Annie Bruneau of Santé Nutrition in Joliette, Quebec, whom I consulted on the topic, briefly explained in the following excerpt the link between energy and healthy eating. She explains clearly and succinctly that caring for your body is one of the best investments you can make.

The link between healthy eating and health has long been proven. Food provides us with the energy and substances that our bodies need to function smoothly. Beyond feeding yourself, which is a basic need to sustain your life, *eating well* is certainly one of the keys to achieving overall physical, mental, and emotional health.

Eating well for energy means taking the time to give the body the energy it needs in the form of meals and snacks by listening to your body's signals to avoid overeating and feeling fatigue afterwards. It also means consuming carbohydrates and proteins every meal. Carbohydrates are our source of fuel and the only source of energy used by the brain. Protein prolongs the feeling of fullness and your energy level between meals. Another way to maintain your energy level is to avoid sweet or refined foods. They provide short-term energy and subsequently cause your energy to drop and fatigue to set in. Excess caffeine can also be a source of fatigue.

This is just some advice. There is more that could be said about it. Making your diet a high priority is an excellent investment. Healthy eating is a key factor in feeling energetic throughout the day. It enables you to enjoyably and effectively perform the day's tasks.

Physical Health

For many years as a younger man, I chased success and forgot to recharge. I did not engage in regular physical activity. When I met successful businesspeople, I was surprised to notice that they included regular physical activity in their daily routine; it was the best way to relieve tension and, above all, recharge their batteries. Successful men and women take care of their physical health and get exercise that keeps them in shape. The greater your responsibilities and plans, the more you should train and take care of your body to bear the burden; otherwise, it may break down. As you know, everyone who does great things is likely to face the most obstacles. It is important to make the decision to take care of yourself through regular physical activity. Whatever activity you choose will be beneficial. Even walking has great effects on your health. People who train their bodies to bear pain have minds that are likely to cope better with adversity.

Testimony

My wife saw an improvement in her morale, well-being, and sexuality when she combined a balanced diet with physical activity.

She drastically changed her lifestyle for a few months. Initially, she just wanted to get back to what she had weighed five years earlier. In the past, she skipped meals without necessarily decreasing the amount she ate; moreover, she was not a sports enthusiast.

She did research on the Internet about losing weight. She said that she had come across various types of diets, but she did not have the willpower to stick to them. Subsequently, she visited forums that talked about the effects of a balanced diet on weight. It was a matter of eating well, not necessarily how much or little you eat. In other words, the suggestions therein focused on experiencing pleasure eating and meeting your needs rather than just eating for pleasure.

In fact, carbohydrates and proteins should each make up a quarter of your plate and vegetables, half. I am not attempting to teach a class on nutrition or dietetics here. I just want to underscore how she changed her relationship with food, her schedules, and the dishes and their quantity. She combined these changes with exercising at the gym, especially swimming. She gradually achieved positive results. She was less out of breath, her libido skyrocketed, and she was in a better mood and more productive at work, not to mention that she actually started regularly losing weight. Her story shows that physical health goes hand in hand with a balanced diet and exercise: They have a direct impact on your energy.

Spiritual Health

Now may the God of peace [...] equip you with everything good
that you may do his will.
—Hebrews 13:21

Prayer is an activity that saved me and brought me closer to God, reinvigorating me in the best way and freeing me from unimaginably dark situations. In Matthew 21:22, it is written, "And whatever you ask in prayer, you will receive, if you have faith."

Activity

This is one of the most important exercises in this book. I invite you to the deepest reflection and discipline, which I hope will lead you to the most important decision in your life: accepting God and letting Him work through you for His glory.

Honestly answer the following questions and figure out how and with whom you want to continue your journey to success:

1. How do you identify yourself?
2. Whom do you call on when the burden is beyond your *capacity*?
3. Do you think you are *capable* of achieving success through your human strength alone? Do you have the means?
4. Do you have faith?

Benefits of Spiritual Health in a Professional Environment

According to Pastor Stéphane Gagné of the Église Baptiste Évangélique Vie nouvelle in Joliette, spiritual health produces healthy motivations for professionals. The reason for your actions will not just be focused on yourself, your earnings, your performance, and your advancement. You will be able to use your God-given gifts and talents to serve others. You will also be able to consider others' interests (Philippians 2:4). As Jesus said, you will experience true joy that way: "It is more blessed to give than to receive" (Acts 20:35).

Spiritual health is characterized by peace in your heart. One of the wounds of our world is spiritual, not medical or viral. Over the years, I have noticed how bitterness, regret, and anger poison the soul. A tremendous heaviness burdens people to the point of diminishing their performance, stealing their joy, and desiccating their inner being. Although skills, the work environment, and physical health are factors that enhance the work you do, the way professionals feel in their heart has a significant effect on their performance.

Spiritual health produces quality relationships. The Bible speaks of forgiveness, humility, the search for good, and reconciliation. God invites people to be at peace, insofar as it depends on them, with their employers and colleagues. This frees the workplace from relational barriers, fosters collaboration, and channels your energies to your tasks and mission.

Spiritual health is characterized by crystal-clear personal convictions. It leads you to know and consistently, meaningfully live by your values. Coherence between what I believe and practice influences the quality of my actions in a clear-cut way; they become less hesitant, wavering, and wayward.

Spiritual health includes a whole range of obstacles, failures, and bankruptcies. Growth does not happen without resistance, opposition, and disappointment. We live in an imperfect, painful, difficult world. But your attitude during adversity sets you apart, this ability to turn obstacles into an opportunity to grow, evolve, and find new avenues that reveal your inner strength. The Bible says that righteous people fall seven times, but they get back up (Proverbs 24:16). A broader perspective than earthly life relativizes failures, deadlines, and even successes.

Regardless of the nature of your project, business, or dream, you are *capable* of the impossible if you follow the steps and take on the leadership role that leads to eternal success. Then pray continually; success belongs only to those who fight for Him through *faith*.

A few years ago, the foundations of my businesses were unsteady because my *faith* was weak. Today I am convinced that my path to success is healthy, certain, and above all, guaranteed. I am now *capable*. Are you?

You have just taken a *step*: progress focused on success.

TO REMEMBER

CHAPTER 7

S UCCESSFUL MEN AND women take care of their physical health and get exercise that keeps them in shape. The greater your responsibilities and plans, the more you should train and take care of your body to bear the burden; otherwise, it may break down. As you know, everyone who does great things is likely to face the most obstacles. It is important to make the decision to take care of yourself through regular physical activity. Whatever activity you choose will be beneficial. Even walking has great effects on your health. People who train their bodies to bear pain have minds that are likely to cope better with adversity.

CONCLUSION

THIS WORK IS intended to be a recipe book for anyone yearning for success. No matter what you do, mastering and applying the concepts in this book will guide your work toward success. You must take one *step* at a time. Having read up to this page, there is one thing that will open the door to success: *starting now*. The best way to fail would be to wait for the right time—there is no right time.

The secret of success is not a matter of your origin, level of education, IQ, or skin color. Applying proven principles, concepts, and laws will be of great help if you long to succeed. Whether you were born rich or poor, here or elsewhere, life will give you what you ask of it based on what you are ready to do to satisfy your heart's desire and deepest thoughts.

The seven eternal laws of success developed here bring together almost two decades of experience in reflecting and working to make my dreams come true. Today I am the product of my thoughts, and more than yesterday, I am ready to achieve the *vision* I had of my life since my awakening.

And you? What is your dream? What is your vision of your life and the world you belong to? Whatever desire lies in your heart, it is important to take the following steps:

1. Acquire KNOWLEDGE, but above all, apply it to develop expertise.
2. Keep a POSITIVE ATTITUDE. The journey will be difficult, and you will need it. Remember, the more you devote yourself to the path to success, the more obstacles you will encounter; the closer you get to it, the heavier the burden.
3. PERSEVERANCE AND PATIENCE are weapons that will undoubtedly lead to success and help you see your work come to fruition. Success can sometimes happen when you least expect it.
4. LOVE elicits, draws, and helps attract love, and without this ingredient, your venture will not be enjoyable, and you will

certainly be dissatisfied even if your project comes to completion. Your success will remain incomplete. Choose to pursue your projects for love, not just for money or acclaim. Love will ensure that your name will continue to be spoken with admiration long after you are gone; in fact, you will never be gone—you will live on in people's minds.

5. The GOAL is the best way not to stray over time; keeping it in mind helps safeguard your work and your project's authenticity. It defines you and makes you who you are; it will determine how the world will remember you. The route will be impossible if your goal is unknown, uncertain, unclear, or open to question. If your *goal* is not clear, stop and define a worthy one.

6. FREEDOM is what you must fight the hardest for. In fact, living freely is more difficult now than in the past. You are directly or indirectly captive of this world, those around you, your fears, and your past. Fight to truly achieve self-fulfillment because that is how you will experience a true feeling of freedom. Whatever people say, whatever they do or do against you and your project, it's all an attempt to dishearten you and undermine your freedom. You are the main actor, the project leader, the business leader. You are the one who will be leaving a mark.

7. ENERGY is crucial to success: it is your engine. Taking care of all facets of your health will help you do more and more, but above all, inspire and convey what you know. Take care of your physical health, eat a healthy diet, and have no reservations about healthy, permissible sex. May the Holy Spirit accompany you and protect you every day. Stay fervent practitioners of the word of God. Draw on it unreservedly, and it will sustain you.

You are now *capable* of success.

Small steps will inevitably lead you to the key to success. It is up to you to open the door to success by practicing its underlying principles. Share this message with a loved one. Take a *step* toward someone. Thank you.

QUOTATIONS AND TOPICS FOR REFLECTION

1. Entrepreneurship is 10 percent inspiration and 90 percent perspiration, but . . .

   Ideas alone are not enough: It takes boldness and determination to turn them into concrete actions that will help make your dream come true. That explains why a handful of people, fewer than 10 percent, holds more than 90 percent of the earth's wealth.

2. The success of a work team comes from the collective individualism of its members, whose common bond is their love for one another—which is called *team spirit*.

   You can measure a team's strength by its weakest link. If each member who comprises it works hard and gives it their best without begrudging the others, the sum of the individual efforts will make the team as good as it can be.

3. Procrastination is a disease whose remedy is the immediate action that goes along with your ideas.

   Putting off what you can do today until tomorrow is a habit that, if it becomes ingrained, will kill your creative genius. Faced with projects, ideas, chores, or even basic daily tasks, you can decide to start working without waiting for the perfect time. One *step* at a time, one *action* after another, one *day* at a time. How many people have died with their projects never having seen the light of day? What would the world be like if everyone let their imagination speak and if those dreams immediately turned into actions? We would certainly live in a better world full of achievement and innovation. You have no control over *tomorrow*. Tomorrow is unforeseeable, but today belongs to you; why put off until tomorrow what can be done today?

4. Waiting for the right time is the best way to fail.

    If the future does not belong to you, how can you wait for the right moment to begin making a change? How can you wait for the right moment if it is unclear? Tomorrow exists if, and only if, today is fully lived and you strive to give it your all as if it were your last day on earth. That way, there will be a tomorrow, regardless of whether you are there.

5. Entrepreneurship is and will forever remain the only way out of unemployment and subservience in the world.

    Imagine a world without businesses, and you will understand that only enterprising people stay completely busy. Entrepreneurship offers the opportunity to manage your time and income. Going into business requires audacity, not absolute control of what you want to get into—everything else will follow.

6. Time and money are luxuries that only the most daring and courageous people in our society have the privilege to experience. The only price to pay is imagining yourself in that situation.

    For the poor and middle class, time is money and money is time. Can you have both? Yes, but there is a tremendous price to pay but not one as tremendous as the courage it takes to imagine yourself there. It costs absolutely nothing to envision an ideal, but not enacting it costs you your life.

7. Achieve financial security, but move toward your financial independence and toward inevitably achieving your financial freedom.

8. If a group of people work together and share a common *vision*, they form a *team* with an extremely high chance of *success*.

9. I am so humble and simple that they think I am naive and stupid: I am a mystery, and I will not change.

10. Do what you can until you become aware of what you should be doing to succeed by doing what you should do.

11. "A good conscience invigorates you. When your mind is freed from inner worries, you can maximize your energy." — Stéphane Gagné

12. "Learn to appreciate differences and the concept of the body, team, and specific roles. Even in major sports competitions, athletes must work together and see diversity as a unifying, productive force. Beware of jealousy and rivalries that hinder project development." — Stéphane Gagné

13. "Find joy in all your actions, not just in their results. Because, in fact, you live more in development than celebration. That way, I will be happy and motivated throughout the process, not waiting to eventually be happy." — Stéphane Gagné

14. "Associate with upright people who, while they may not be perfect, have demonstrated honor and maturity. Because what is often lacking in a company is not talent or resources but ethical strength." — Stéphane Gagné

15. Accept defeat, but above all, refuse to give up, and you will achieve *success*.

16. Avoid distraction agents—television, the Internet, popular newspapers, and social networks—and you will be free.

17. Discipline is learned from an early age; it develops over time.

NOTES

NOTES

NOTES

NOTES

CPSIA information can be obtained
at www.ICGtesting.com
Printed in the USA
BVHW071911160720
583883BV00001B/172